"Reflection is such an important part of the teaching process, and teachers need to be mindful of what we do in our classrooms, why we do it, and whether or not it is working.

"Teachers are not only charged with teaching their content areas but they also have the responsibility of shaping their students into being the best humans that they can be.... These chapters remind me of the important work that we must do in our classrooms each day."

– Lindsey M. Jones
2nd Grade Teacher, Nashville, Tennessee

"I must say that this is enjoyable reading for me. This book contains a plethora of great experiences…"
– Sonia Mitchell
Executive Director Retired, Miami, Florida

"[This book] tackled the subject of safety in a very relatable way. I want to make the Mateo child in our school feel safe. Great personal touch by sharing your testimonies of the painful marks."

– Jeff Hendred
Middle School Principal, Ottumwa Iowa

Leave a Mark!

*8 ways to help your
students become
their best selves*

Connie S. Johnson

Rufus D. Stephens

Printed in the United States of America
ISBN 978-1-946425-91-1

Book Design by CSinclaire Write-Design
Cover Design by Klevur

• WRITE WAY •
PUBLISHING COMPANY
RALEIGH, NORTH CAROLINA
www.writewaypublishingcompany.com

DEDICATION

To the unsung heroes of learning . . . TEACHERS. Whatever the grade level, they bring impact and transformation for which the world is far better.

And to my three greatest blessings, my husband and children. Craig, thank you for going along with all of my harebrained ideas. You are a great sounding board. You bring the much needed practicality to my creativity. Thank you for letting me be me. I am forever grateful. To my not so little "little people," it is one of my greatest joys to be your mom. You each inspire and challenge me to be better. Of all the marks I may leave on this world, I hope that the greatest ones are left on you.

– Constance S. Johnson, M.Ed. School Counseling

In memory of the educator of educators, my mother, Mattie Stephens, and to my wife, Cynthia, whose patience and encouragement were inestimable, and to my "hall of friends," who were forever cheering us on in this endeavor.

– Rufus D. Stephens, Motivational Speaker & Author

Contents

Foreword ix

Acknowledgments xi

Introduction 1

The "A" Team 4

The Case for Educators 7

The Painful Marks 10

The Mark of Visibility 17

The Mark of Accountability 30

The Mark of Listening 38

The Mark of Empowerment 46

The Mark of Caring 56

The Mark of Belonging 63

The Mark of Safety 72

The Hill You've Chosen 79

Something to Think About 82

About the Author - Constance 84

About the Author - Rufus 85

FOREWORD

I remember the moment I walked into my own classroom for the very first time. The excitement was high, and the questions racing across my mind were many. Will my students even like me? Will I be able to teach them all the required standards? How can I make a positive impact on their lives? Will my students know that they are loved and accepted in my classroom? What will the parents think of me? What do I do when I make a mistake? The questions went on and on, and 16 years later, now as a school counselor, I find myself still asking these same questions at the beginning of every new school year.

As educators, we greatly desire to do what is best for our students, and we are met with numerous obstacles that can make that goal difficult to reach at times. Nonetheless, staying in a constant state of self-awareness and self-reflection allows us to grow in our craft. It pushes us to take the necessary steps to provide quality instruction layered with compassion and to build sincere rapport with our students with hopes of leaving an impression that will last a lifetime.

Leave A Mark! gives us that push we need to keep reflecting and growing in our field. It helps us to remember why we do what we do each day and to see our students as impressionable human beings that need to be loved, treated with dignity, and challenged to excel. It reminds us to see the whole individual, beyond the classroom doors, and to offer a smile, warmth, and understanding when it is desperately needed. It causes us to evaluate our personal biases and make choices that will expand our influence with our students and colleagues. It also validates our efforts, the countless hours no one knows about that we spend to ensure our students receive our best every time.

I thank my dear friend Connie for sharing this remarkable book with me and for allowing me to write a few words to you. When you have completed this book, may you walk away as I did: inspired, encouraged, and challenged. I am reminded of Deuteronomy 32:2, *"Let my teaching drop as the rain, my speech distill as the dew, as the droplets on the fresh grass and as the showers on the herb."* Let us use these tools that Connie and Rufus have shared to provide the rain our students need to bloom and shine.

– Renita Matthews M.Ed.
Certified School Counselor

ACKNOWLEDGMENTS

To the phenomenal educators that I have had the privilege of caring for kids alongside. Every school has its own culture, and the ones that I have been blessed to serve in have all helped to shape me as a person and an educator. It is truly an honor to currently work among a compilation of some of education's greatest assets. I am proud to be a member of the Westcliff family. Observing you, laboring alongside you, and knowing you inside and outside of the classroom has had a positive impact on me. In relationship to our noble profession, you are each the embodiment of the verse "As iron sharpens iron so one man sharpens another." I am grateful for your sharpening.

– Connie

Leave a Mark!

INTRODUCTION

Teachers make all other professions possible.
— Anonymous

Working for salaries that are nowhere commensurate with their skillsets or their deliverables, teachers answer their professional call every day! If teachers were granted the opportunity to get a glimpse into the future and see the effect they had on their students, they would be astounded. Living proofs come in all sizes, colors, voices, and ethnicities. The world at large is better on so many levels because of committed teachers. One Japanese proverb says, *"Better than a thousand days of diligent study is one day with a great teacher."*

Teachers bring light, understanding, possibilities, and encouragement to students who will one day change the world. Teachers mold thought, unlock talents, expand minds, and often provide safety for some of their students when that safety exists nowhere else in the world. Teachers have the awesome opportunity to speak into the lives of large groups of the next generation. They have the unique ability to edit someone else's life story.

Henry Adams said, *"A teacher affects eternity: [they] can never tell where [their] influence stops."* Educators are among the most essential professionals in the world. Teachers bring commitment, passion, heart, and skillsets to their students, class after class, and year after year.

Educators have always been revered in our family. Celebrated in the book *Life Lessons from Miss Mattie,* Mattie Stephens, family matriarch, set the drumbeat for excellence in education. Of Miss Mattie's five children, three became exemplary educators. Had she lived, she would have been enormously proud that one of her granddaughters entered a new generation of educators.

In today's challenging and changing times, our education system has felt many repercussions from the events, yet teachers have found ways to continue to reach out to their students, to teach them, counsel them, and align the trajectory for success in their lives. We've written this book to support you, salute you, and hopefully to encourage you to continue to leave your special marks on students. We hope the experiences we share, the case studies, and the chapter reflections will pour over you to give you strength and inspiration to continue the wonderful work that you do.

For those of you seeking to separate our voices, there sometimes are hints! I, Rufus, have two daughters, one of whom is Connie, the co-author of this book, and I have exceeded seven decades of living and am enjoying life these days as a public speaker and an ordained minister.

I, Connie, have a son and a daughter and am, as noted, an educator with both classroom and counseling experience.

We wrote this book together from basic principles we hold. We write as one voice but from different experiences. We have not only experienced it ourselves but time and time again have seen how much influence teachers have with their students and what marks they can make. What we wish is to help you—encourage you—to make the marks you leave good ones.

THE "A" TEAM

*Excellence is to do a common thing
in an uncommon way.*
— Booker T. Washington

As you are too well aware, an enemy came on our shores in early 2020. The virulent COVID-19 virus would transform reality as we knew it. One of the hardest hit and disrupted areas of our society is that of education.

New designations were coined to describe this different reality that educators would be forced to confront. Learning options were established and termed "virtual learning" and "in-person learning." For millennia, in most cases, learning had been an "in-person" proposition. How else would you teach kids? Well, the pandemic would force some productive creativity from committed educators to create a new teaching model. Many districts wrestled and still wrestle with whether to have in-person or virtual learning. Some decided on a hybrid of the two, and learning happened and is still happening in that modified reality.

This chapter celebrates educators who showed up at the COVID battlefront with their A games. While academics may have taken place with virtual learning, students suffered in a key area. One of the biggest negative impacts was the lack of student socialization. Research indicates that students suffer demonstrably because of not being able to be with their teachers and fellow students.

Enter the A game educators! One educator missed her students and knew they missed her. She decided that once a week, she would drive to her students' homes and pay them a visit. Properly masked and socially distanced, she would show up at her students' residences and let them know how they were missed. Her act of kindness reaped huge dividends.

Consider another of our A gamers. This committed educator facilitates learning in a hybrid fashion with both in-person and virtual learning. Aware of her students' longing and need for socialization, she provides moments of connection in a very creative way. She pans the room with the computer camera allowing both the virtual and in-person learners to experience moments of connection. You can just imagine the joy of her students as a friend's face appears on the board. Connection does not have to be long, it just has to be.

In another instance, an entire grade level team brought their A game. When teachers returned to the building though all students remained virtual, teachers continued to teach. As teachers taught, the fire alarm sounded signaling the need to evacuate as part of the mandatory monthly fire drill. These teachers didn't miss a beat as they transferred their virtual meetings to their phones and continued teaching as they evacuated the building. One teacher was seen pronouncing the spelling words for a test as he went.

These are three examples of teachers who validated the old saying that "Necessity is the mother of invention." All across America, educators are rising to the occasion of the onslaught of this unrelenting virus. They stay true to their mission, and our children get educated, even if in a compromised reality. We salute the innovators!

THE CASE FOR EDUCATORS

A good teacher is like a candle,
it consumes itself to light the way for others.
— Giovanni Ruffini

Why did you choose to go into education? We think it is safe to say that it was not simply for income. No, you desired something more meaningful. Before becoming a teacher, many of you dreamed about the students whose lives you would change for the better.

You would watch great educator movies like *Lean on Me, Dangerous Minds, Stand and Deliver*, and *The Freedom Writers*, and you would wonder what the box office hit honoring you would be titled. You don't expect every day to be great, but you do want to leave an impact. Leaving an impact is why past students return to say "Hi" or tell stories about you without you knowing.

True educators seek to leave marks that change the entire trajectory of a student's life and that of their families. They do it in an effort to make their world a better place. They drink their coffee, grade papers on the weekend, visit TPT (Teachers Pay Teachers), and spend their own money on school supplies. They jam themselves into small rooms with 20 or more students, and talk their non-teacher friends' ears off about their "kids."

You came into this profession with intentionality and that is exactly what all the great educators have done. The greater your focus on that intention, the greater the impact you will leave. You can probably think of teachers over your educational career who drove you toward choosing to become a teacher either because they were such great teachers that you wanted to emulate them or maybe because they weren't so great, and you knew students deserved better.

And then came COVID-19. It is that same intentionality that has enabled you to weather the storm of COVID. The old reality had you looking into your students' welcoming and sometimes not so welcoming faces every day. In either case, some degree of learning happened. Then COVID-19 showed up and overturned what both you and your students called "normal."

But true to your calling and ends-orientation, you monitored and adjusted. Virtual learning became the order of the day. It was challenging and ran at right angles to the social needs and familiar surroundings of the learning place you knew. Still, you rose to the occasion. You pushed past new teaching platforms, attendance inconveniences, and fears of COVID-19 to affect learning. You now stand proudly to the benefit of your students and the district with whom you've allied yourself.

Whether you are a first year teacher building your own classroom experiences or a teacher who has taught for years, you are honoring your calling and doing what educators are meant to do . . . **leave a mark!**

THE PAINFUL MARKS

~Rufus~

Words can inspire and words can destroy.
Choose yours well.

— Robin Sharma

The thing about marks is that they come with and without painful reflections. My junior high and high school years revealed a fair share of painful marks. Here I am now over 70 years old reflecting on these impactful and painful marks left by teachers who either chose a wrong career path or had long since outlived the passion that originally drew them to education.

This story from my elementary school could be called "Rush to Judgment."

I was in 4th grade, and I got into a tiff with a girl and was sent to the principal's office. The

10

principal sent me home where I was immediately and significantly punished by my grandmother, who was amazed to see me walk through the door at mid-morning.

Something like three weeks later, our 4th grade class had a substitute teacher filling in for our regular teacher. When we were lining up for lunch, I simply touched a friend on the shoulder to ask him a question. Unfortunately for me, I caught him on a bad day, and he told the substitute that I was bothering him. Not wishing to hear of my innocence, she immediately sent me to the principal's office. Yep, you heard it right; same principal. The principal saw me coming down the hall and simply said, "Go home, Stephens." Not believing what had just happened, I made my way home where my loving grandmother believed me and didn't punish me.

By all accounts, I was innocent. But I suffered the embarrassment and was the victim of misapplied justice that I'm still talking about six decades later. It would have been so easy for the principal to ask a couple of questions to realize that I had done nothing wrong. This story illustrates how educators can all too easily leave painful marks.

I remember another such teacher, another "leaver" of painful marks. The teacher taught algebra, and I was in her 9th grade class. I wasn't a bad student. Admittedly, I probably talked too much sometimes.

Because of my upbringing and because I came from a family of teachers, I could never be disrespectful. However, I still managed to get solidly in her cross-hairs. One time in particular sticks in my mind.

It was time for mid-term exams. I was not a great student in math, and I didn't expect to do well. My grade reflected the challenge that Algebra presented for me. On a particular day, the teacher returned our papers and proceeded to announce each student's name and grade.

I can still hear her now as she called my name, "Stephens, D minus." That alone was like a punch in the gut. Imagine the insult to injury scenario when she added with the sharpest edge in her tone, "I wanted to give you an F, but I had to give you the D minus." Of course the class went up in an uproar. Remember this was 9th grade. Anything could be the source humor resulting in great embarrassment.

This teacher had been teaching for many years. She obviously should have realized on some level that her behavior served no one well. She left a mark, but unfortunately it was one of the painful ones.

I have repeated this story more times than I can count. When I think of the mission of a teacher, the task they all sign up for and the passion that should be there until the mission is over, I am saddened by painful marks like these. I also consider how easy it would have been for that teacher to sidestep leaving that mark. The possibilities were endless.

Another painful mark, though more subtle, that teachers can make unwittingly is active exclusion in the classroom. Let us make our point. Classrooms are made up of students with varying academic skills. There are the stars, the students who have rarely earned anything less than an "A" all of their academic lives.

Then there are the students at the other end of the spectrum—the "bottomers" for lack of a kinder designation. Those students' grades hang in the C minus and lower range. Then finally, there are the "tweeners." These are B & C students. Teachers can unwittingly defer to the "stars" when asking questions. They make two erroneous assumptions. First, they assume that the star is always going to have the right answer. On some strange and irrational level, they seek to be appreciated by the "stars," a source of validation of their teaching skills.

Second, they assume that the "tweeners" and "bottomers" won't ever have the right answers. For a student, there is nothing like knowing the answer and being denied the opportunity to share it. Teachers who do this fail to realize the painful marks they leave. When teachers unwittingly form this caste system within their classrooms, they can negatively impact a student's self-image and potential for future success.

Consider the story of Shantram Hawkins, Doctor of Educational Leadership. He outran the negative predictions around his life but not without sustaining painful marks along the way. In his reflection of school life, he listed the negative and painful things said about him. He lists these predictions people made relating to his life possibilities:

1. He will be another Black male statistic.

2. He's an academic failure.

3. He's another child without a father figure. He'll be a menace to society.

4. His elementary school principal told his mama that he wouldn't finish high school.

5. He was teased for having to be pulled out of class for IEP services.

6. Teachers said that he wouldn't be able to pass the Louisiana high school exit exam to receive a high school diploma.

7. He was told he would never be able to go to college or enter military services.

Shantram didn't just receive a single painful mark, but rather he received a barrage of them! You can easily see how receiving painful marks like these can have students play to the predictions and become what was being said about them. He, however, overcame the predictions and proved them false.

Your job as a teacher is, by far, one of the most difficult professions in the world. And yet it can also be the most rewarding and most impactful, if executed well.

Perhaps you have left a painful mark on a student's life unawares. It is our sincere hope that the stories shared here will cause you to reflect on your classroom practices. If you realize that you're inflicting a negative impact, be thankful you caught it now. Your next move is to figure out a way to reverse it. We believe that if the people in these stories had known the negative impact they would have on their students, they would have chosen a way to leave better marks. Mary Hatwood Futrell said, "When the untapped potential of a student meets the liberating art of a teacher, a miracle unfolds."

CHAPTER REFLECTIONS

In this chapter on "Painful Marks," what was most impactful for you?

_____

_____

_____

How will you remain aware of the potential to leave painful marks?

_____

_____

_____

What is one step you will take to make certain you leave no painful marks?

_____

_____

_____

THE MARK OF VISIBILITY

~Connie~

*What we really yearn for as human beings
is to be visible.*

Jacqueline Novograt

You have probably played the game of hide and seek or observed it at some point in your life. The object of this game, as you know, is not to be found or seen by the person who is "it." I would venture to say that playing this game and maybe a few others like it are the few times in life when we desire *not* to be seen. Sure, some superhero enthusiasts dream of possessing the power of invisibility. For most of us though, in any real relationships we have had, we never wanted to be invisible. Instead, we desired to be, and we were, seen.

Think about the person who makes you feel seen.

They don't even have to look at you to accomplish the task. They understand you. They acknowledge you. They know what makes you tick, what excites you, and what angers you. It is what makes all relationships, even those between teachers and students, worth having.

Like in archery, you must keep your eyes open and trained on your target in order to have any chance of hitting it. Before you can leave a mark on your student, you must first see your student. Of course this is more than simply noting, almost unthinkingly, that "Marcus" is present. This is about seeing that Marcus is more tired today than normal, a bit melancholy, grumpy, or down right despondent.

As the younger of two, I was constantly referred to by teachers who taught my sister as "Monica's sister." Even outside of school I was sometimes referred to in the duo of "Monica and Connie." Normally, it didn't bother me. I can assure you though, the teachers who assumed that they knew me because they knew my sister will not be listed in my former teachers hall of fame. Those teachers never took the time to get to know me.

It's natural to classify things, even helpful in some situations. But we do ourselves well by not treating our students as a set of silverware. I'm guilty of falling into this habit occasionally myself. It doesn't work so well with people. If you know anyone at all, then you know that family of origin does not necessarily dictate similarity.

Handling visibility is an intentional act of the will. It takes an extra moment before or after you dive into the rigor of the content for you to acknowledge each student as an individual. The practice of door greetings makes this a bit easier to accomplish. One way to enhance this practice is by asking a check-in question each morning while taking care to call students by name. If it is a unique name, you may be the only person who pronounces it correctly that day. There is an old saying that says, *"The sweetest sound to everyone is the sound of their own name."*

One way that the mark of visibility can be underscored is through intentionally seeing the student through the lens of ethnicity. Often, well-meaning people say things like "I don't see color." The meaning behind that, in the best of cases, is I don't treat you differently based on the color of your skin. That should definitely be the truth for all teachers. But if I don't see color, then I don't see you both literally and figuratively. Yeah, it's that deep. Ignoring our ethnic and cultural differences limits the ability for each of us to show up as our authentic selves.

As a teenager I took two African American history classes as my electives, not because I didn't know much about the content, but to feel as though my culture mattered. In truth, I knew it mattered because my parents celebrated our heritage and encouraged me to be comfortable in my own skin.

I took many history classes throughout my educational career, but the stories of people who looked like me and my other classmates of color, with the exception of Martin Luther King Jr., Rosa Parks, and Cesar Chavez, were noticeably absent. I sought out these African American history classes to fill in the gap.

When I completed the classes, the gap still remained. One class consisted of the story of Tina Turner's life which included a book study of her autobiography and the viewing of *What's Love Got to Do with It*. We also participated in a "soul food" potluck. The other class was simply a continuous watching of *Eyes on the Prize* videos. Some of those things were good, but they left me looking for more. It was at that time that I began to think about the cultures of my other minority peers since there were no history classes that focused on their ethnicities. I was convinced that there should be a mandatory multicultural class in which students would learn about the cultures of all students, specifically students of color. I was dead set on making it happen one day when I became a teacher.

Now that I have spent some time in the world of education, I think I was a bit off base. Ethnicity is not something that people of color can compartmentalize or take off between 6th and 7th period. It is who we are. So, we as educators can't simply require a mandatory class. It does our students no good for them to feel seen racially for 30 days of the year or even 45 minutes of each day. We as educators have the opportunity, privilege, and, if I may push further, the responsibility to seek out books, media, and even math problems that elevate and celebrate children of all ethnicities.

Here's an even deeper challenge. If you work on a majority minority campus, don't only supplement curriculum materials that celebrate the majority of the students on your campus. Celebrate them all. My son talked to me about one of his high school history teachers celebrating many cultures. This small but meaningful act caused him to have a deeper appreciation for the contributions of people of his own ethnicity as well as those of other cultures and races.

This isn't easy, I know. We must be intentional about incorporating the stories from all ethnicities but especially those of minority groups. This can be tricky because no one wants to be seen as the eternal underdog where every story about their people group is of some struggle for equality that they should have simply because they exist. Those stories must be told, but told in an effort to truly see our students. These stories cannot be the Alpha and Omega of what we teach our students about people outside of the majority culture.

If you teach history, the opportunities are boundless to teach the truth about history and challenge your scholars to think critically. If you teach English/ Language Arts, then look for books by diverse authors in which the main characters are representative of a variety of ethnicities. If math or science is your specialty, highlight the discoveries of mathematicians and scientists across cultures. Katherine Johnson, Pedro Nunes, Abu Ja'Far Mohammad, Flossie Wong-Staal, Fred Begay, Benjamin Banneker, St. Elmo Brady, Victor Neumann-Lara, E. K. Janika Ammal, Maraym Mirzakhani, Mayly Sanchez, and Valerie Thomas are wonderful places to start.

Make sure to include a variety of different people who aren't deceased from each ethnic group and representatives of a variety of countries, because people groups are not monolithic cultures; there are many contributors to choose from in every ethnic group. As you would expect, students can relate better to those who are still alive. Some of you may be wondering whether I ever really taught after making suggestions like these, as though you don't have enough to do. Trust me, I've been there. I am still there in a different capacity, but I urge you to go the extra mile because it matters.

If we continue to use only the curriculum that is adopted by our districts, we run the risk not only of failing to leave this very important mark but worse yet, leaving a painful mark of invisibility. That mark tells students who are not embraced and celebrated that they don't matter, that their thoughts, views, and contributions don't matter. It affects not only their feelings toward themselves but also toward those who look like them. It supports the narrative that the majority culture is better and that in order to matter, they must conform and make themselves invisible.

Giving equal time to shine, conversely, helps fight against shame that some minority students may feel from being treated differently. It helps cultivate a culture of empathy and celebration for everyone. It can foster a true understanding of differences that cause us as teachers to be more effective as advocates for the young lives we shape.

I remember teaching a classroom counseling lesson once. I often joke about feeling like a comedian in my approach. Before I begin, I always have to "feel out the crowd." In one lesson shortly before the Thanksgiving holiday, I was polling the students about what they were most looking forward to about the upcoming holiday. My focus was on the food. I was in a dual-language classroom. I know there are many models for this learning style, but on my campus these students are bilingual with a dominant language of Spanish. Many of the families in this class were very much in tune with their heritage and culture. So as I stood before the students asking about turkey and various pies, the excitement that was shown during the beginning of our discussion began to wane.

Finally, one student raised her hand to tell me that her family would have tamales. As if set free by her honesty, other hands shot up proclaiming that they would eat menudo and posole and various desserts. With understanding, I smiled and continued our banter. You had better believe that I didn't lead with turkey in the next dual-language classroom.

Today, I probably wouldn't be as presumptuous as to assume that everyone was joyfully celebrating this holiday to begin with. I have no shame. Tell me what I don't know. But now that I know better, the onus is on me to do better. Modeling this and creating space for everyone teaches all students that they do not need to dim the lights of others so that they can shine.

We tend to distance ourselves from what seems strange or unfamiliar to us. Doing this denies us the opportunities to experience the richness that cultures unlike our own have to offer. The concern surrounding inequality toward people of color has become nearly impossible to avoid in recent months. As educators, let's use our unique position as influencers in an effort to interrupt systems of inequality starting with our classrooms.

That Kid

Acknowledging our students and the many nuances that make them who they are does not end with their ethnicity. I am reminded of my early years of teaching. I was working in a school where student behavior was a noticeable challenge. When we were "pitching classes," behavior was one of the main factors that determined which students were placed in which classes.

On one occasion, in the middle of the school year, a student who had previously attended the school was rumored to be returning. The students were overjoyed, but the staff clearly had different emotions. After some discussion, the decision was made that this student would be a part of my team because the entire teaching staff on my team was new to the campus and had not had any previous experience managing his behavior.

A few days after his return, but before any major disciplinary incidents, the teachers, administration, and this young boy met to discuss expectations and his needs in a desire to keep everything calm. At one point during the discussion, the boy fondly remembered Ms. Warrenbeck, one of his teachers from the previous year. He reported that he did get into trouble in her class from time to time, but not like in other classes. When asked why, his response was impactful. He said, "She likes me. I'm like her favorite student."

I wondered if she would have described him in those same words, but one thing is certain; he felt seen in that classroom. He wasn't just another student labeled solely by his behavior in her class, and he knew it. His needs were met in that classroom, and he did not deem it necessary to meet them himself through disruption. As I recounted what made the difference for him, one administrator shared that all of the students felt that way—that they were her favorite.

I don't know if she was made aware of either of those conversations, but her actions had a lasting effect not just on that boy but on the other students in her class and on her peers. As you'll remember, I noted that the students were overjoyed to hear that this boy was returning to school with them. Her acknowledgment of him as a multi-dimensional person affected his behavior and the way that he was viewed by his classmates.

As a relatively new teacher and specifically new to the grade level that I was teaching, his words stuck with me. To have the student who notoriously struggled to regulate his emotions and behavior speak about a teacher in such a positive light, that teacher must be doing something right. Without even knowing it, she challenged me to start each day anew and see the complexity in every student.

Later, I found myself challenged by another student who had a lot to say. I found myself often corralling her outbursts. She always had something thought-provoking to say. That was great unless I was in the middle of teaching or the class was supposed to be working quietly. During independent practice time, she would hold court with those closest to her. She would complete her assignments, but her classmates weren't always as fortunate.

One day in the heat of a discussion, I called her to my desk and said, "Monique, you know what?" With too much attitude, which I chose to ignore, she responded "Yes." I continued, "You know who you remind me of?" Certain that it would not be a flattering comparison, she looked down and said, "Who?" "Me, at 11 or 12," I replied. Her face lit up.

I shared how I too had a lot to say, and it was a challenge for me to learn when and where not to speak. I also tacked on that while she was smart and a good student, her discussions made it hard for some of her peers to keep up. It was my attempt at a "teachery" "I see you, girl!" moment. From that day on she made a noticeable effort to curb her off-task discussions. Had I not been influenced by Ms. Warrenbeck, I may not have operated with such grace.

Of all of the ways to leave a mark of visibility, I chose perhaps one of the most difficult. Seeing that kid. In the world of counseling, we focus a lot on identifying the need behind the behavior. If we can meet the need, we can change the behavior. That sounds great in a textbook and even in an undergraduate classroom, but it is a true test of wills when you are in the classroom day in and day out. Even if you are a student teacher, you can probably name the one or two or three that challenge you and the classroom. The trick is to find out what the need is behind the behavior. Could *that* kid just need to be seen?

CHAPTER REFLECTIONS

In this chapter on "Visibility," what was most impactful for you?

_____

_____

_____

What steps will you take to make certain that your students feel "seen" and ultimately appreciated in your classroom?

_____

_____

_____

What tool could you use to remind yourself of the importance of student visibility?

_____

_____

_____

THE MARK OF ACCOUNTABILITY

~Connie~

If you want children to keep their feet on the ground,
put some responsibility on their shoulders.
– Abigail Van Buren

"A half-truth is a whole lie." These words, echoing in the hallway stopped me from completing the task on my computer and drew me toward the doorway so that I could listen more closely. These words were uttered by my friend and the teacher whose classroom was closest to my office. I peeked out to see her having a discussion with one of her students. She was the 5th grade Science teacher. You couldn't be promoted out of elementary school without her having the opportunity to make an impact on your life.

She loved her students, and they loved her, not just

because she was fun and made Science exciting but also because they knew she would not allow them to self-destruct. This wasn't the first time I heard her speaking with a student about a poor choice they had made, and it was far from the last.

She lovingly held her students accountable. I'm not sure that they would have used that term, but they knew she cared. Because she cared, they worked hard for her and received her corrections. I'm sure that they did not enjoy the hallway chats, but they were better because of them. I know this because they return year after year with or without younger siblings to various school events in search of Mrs. Morrison.

The mark of accountability is one that you may shy away from if you have ever struggled in the world of people-pleasing as I have. I have found, however, that holding people accountable is the best way to please them in the long run. Accountability is necessary for adults as well as children. We set our students up for success in life if they can get this thing called accountability. The goal is discipline. Unfortunately, we often confuse discipline with punishment. Punishment is punitive, but discipline is designed to change behavior.

Now, if you have been in the classroom for any amount of time, you realize that discipline is necessary. You also realize that sometimes discipline comes with a punishment or consequence. Lest I lead you to believe that I think punishment is never appropriate and have you slam the book shut, let me explain further.

If Peggy does not do her homework and Peggy is punished by not being allowed to enjoy recess, Peggy will miss recess. She may or may not complete her homework during that time. There is no guarantee, however, that Peggy will begin completing her homework regularly, which is the desired result.

Peggy should have a consequence for her choice not to do her work. But a consequence in isolation leads to contempt at worst and meaningless compliance at best. One successful end to Peggy's story includes a conversation that helps Peggy plan for a pattern of completed assignments in the future while she sits out during recess. Teachers who seek to go deeper to reach Peggy bring her to a place of accountability where compliance is a pleasant by-product.

Leaving the mark of accountability doesn't just happen the day that Peggy doesn't complete her homework. It begins the day that Peggy first meets her teacher. Accountability requires relationship in order to be effective.

Think about the last time someone corrected you. Did you receive that correction? How easy was it for you to do so? How long did that take? I am willing to bet that the time it took for you to receive and act on that correction is in direct correlation to the strength of your relationship with the person who offered the critique. Kids are not much different.

Accountability is much like your checking account. It will hurt when you write a big check, taking out a significant amount of your funds, but it will hurt less if you have made deposits prior to a major withdrawal. In a teacher-student relationship, the overdraft fees look like distance, contempt, or some unkind words about you on a bathroom stall.

Building a relationship doesn't mean ignoring poor choices or misbehavior. Instead it looks like taking an interest in what interests a student. Learning about what home is like for them and appropriately sharing about your life. Attending a sports game or recital if invited. Building relationships doesn't have to be this formal though. Intentionally taking a few minutes to have a one-on-one conversation in passing can go a long way.

Building a relationship looks like leaving their dignity intact when they make an academic mistake. This all sets the groundwork for when you will have to correct their behavior. You take them to a place where you can address them privately, and you call out the misbehavior and follow it with a discussion about better choices. You allow them to experience the consequences of their actions. You teach them to problem solve in the future, which leads to changed behavior.

Another teacher mastered this skill and its effects continue to reverberate in the life of a former student some three and a half decades later. My sister tells the story of being a mischievous nine year old. Having seen the chair pulled out from under someone on one of her favorite television shows, she decided to try it herself. Her classmates didn't respond with laughter as the studio audience had. The teacher certainly responded differently, sternly correcting my sister for her choice of action that hurt one of her classmates.

That conversation had an impact on my sister because she liked Mrs. Carpenter and had not intended to upset her by her actions. She also knew that Mrs. Carpenter would not allow her or her classmates to get away with such misbehavior. After the punishment was doled out and the apology issued and accepted, my sister went home and thought about her actions.

She was so moved that she returned to school the next day and apologized to her entire class for her actions the day before. Another student, an innocent bystander, gave her a hug afterward. It was the culture of love that Mrs. Carpenter fostered in her classroom that allowed that hug and later a strong friendship to develop between my sister and the girl who was hurt.

Mrs. Carpenter taught her students that they could make mistakes and still receive love, even in discipline. "That classroom was filled with love because she loved each of us," my sister said, remembering her 4th grade year fondly.

My father, Rufus, also shares an impactful story of an accountability mark left on him by his 12th grade teacher. These are his words.

I was walking down the hall during the passing period. My mind was focused only on getting to my next class. It was altogether a pretty good day. It wouldn't stay that way much longer.

As I passed my homeroom teacher's class, a fellow classmate, ever the practical joker, stepped on the heel of my shoe. My forward motion caused me to walk out of my shoe. Before I knew it, I swore— loudly! As though the universe converged on me at that exact moment, I found myself in the doorway of my homeroom class.

Although I was walking past her classroom, there was more than enough time for this profane shout to be heard by my homeroom teacher, Mrs. Lane. She just happened to be working at her desk at that very moment. Mrs. Lane was the quintessential educator. She was truly a teaching professional.

When I looked at Mrs. Lane, I knew I couldn't run

away. Besides that, I actually felt embarrassed. I entered the room where Mrs. Lane, still standing at her desk, continued working. I walked slowly around the perimeter of the room toward her. It was one of the longest walks of my life—a "Green Mile" type of walk. When I reached her desk, I simply said, "Mrs. Lane , I'm sorry."

It was at this point that her professionalism and mark-leaving ability shone brightly. Her response was brief but incredibly impactful. She looked at me and said, "Stephens, you should never have to apologize for using profanity." After that, she was done. And so was I.

The relationship that he had with Mrs. Lane forced him to face her. She held him accountable simply with one look. Accountability only happens when the necessary discipline is blended with a caring heart and a desire for better behavior from the student. When accountability is done well, it is translated to the student as love.

CHAPTER REFLECTIONS

In this chapter on "Accountability," what was most impactful for you?

_____

_____

_____

What stories, life lessons, or games could you incorporate to instill accountability in your students?

_____

_____

_____

We all respond well to those things that benefit us; your students are no different. What learning tool will you use to illustrate the benefits of accountability in your students?

_____

_____

_____

THE MARK OF LISTENING

~Connie~

*Listening is an art that requires attention
over talent, spirit over ego, others over self.*
— Dean Jackson

In an effort to be introspective, I occasionally discuss my parenting with my children. They have frequent critiques that I endure. On one occasion when I was speaking to my son, I told him that I try to listen to both his and his sister's point of view. I explained that even though I hear them out, I have to make the final decisions that are best for them. At one point in our exchange, he stopped me dead in my tracks. He referenced a discussion we'd had earlier and said, "That [discussion] showed me that my thoughts and what I say don't matter."

I quickly and passionately responded by telling

him that I would never say something like that to him. He said, "No, you didn't say it. But the result of that interaction made me feel like what I said and how I felt didn't matter." My reaction—Whoa! Major mom fail! That was never my intention! What now? Driven by compassion and the desire to keep the lines of communication open, my response was, "You're right, I blew it there. That was not what I meant to express to you." I even put myself out there and gave him permission to remind me of this encounter if I over-talked him in the future, gently and respectfully of course.

Much like parents, teachers must make the final decisions, but we must also be active listeners. Listeners who do not simply audibly acknowledge what our students say but effect change based on what they say. With my son, I heard him but didn't allow his perspective to change my course of action, leading him to believe that he didn't matter and that I didn't listen to him.

From my childhood, I remember the teacher reviewing the rules that she or he had written on the first day of school each year. Most of the rules started with "don't" and focused on what the student needed to do in order to show respect to the teacher, their peers, and even the classroom. By the time I began teaching, the school of thought shifted some, and we were encouraged to write the rules with our students on the first day of school.

It was drilled into my head at that time to make sure the rules did not start with a negative but instead focused on the desired behavior. For example: "walk" instead of "no running." I still find myself using that one word to redirect students when I am monitoring the hallways. While the method for creating rules changed from the time when I was a student until I became a teacher, the focus was always on the behavior of the students.

In more recent years, the creation of the classroom rules has changed dramatically. The rules aren't just for the students but for all members of the classroom—yes, the teacher too—as citizens working together in a community. Restorative Practices, derived from Restorative Justice principles, have introduced the respect agreement to teachers today. This method focuses on helping students learn that their actions have consequences for them and others, and when they blow it, they must seek to restore what was destroyed by their actions. The best way to teach is to model.

The respect agreement has teachers work together with students to create a finished product that details what respect looks like from student to teacher, student to student, everyone to the environment, and even the teacher to the student. While this may be mandated in some schools and never revisited, it sets the stage for the first day of school. It says "tell me what you need from me." It communicates that respect from a teacher to their students is the norm and not an exception.

Depending on the age of the students, the teacher may need to curb the suggestions that the students have, but it provides students with the unspoken expectation that they can be free to be both seen and heard in this classroom.

Why does this matter? Certainly it is possible to teach content to students without setting the stage for open communication. It is important to listen because there are times when they will have a decision to make, and they will need a sounding board. I once taught a 6th grader who said to me, "Mrs. Johnson, can I talk to you? I need to talk to someone who's not eleven years old." Sure our students don't always ask for our two cents, but it's nice for them to know they have a trusted adult to go to if they need one.

The Circle Up

One way to encourage and foster the skill of listening in ourselves and others is to practice it. One aspect of the restorative practices model is to have what is called a circle. The circle may be initiated for a variety of reasons. Students may initiate a circle to discuss an issue that has arisen in the classroom, whether for the entire community or just for a few students that are affected.

Administrators may initiate a circle including all

members who are involved in an incident that resulted in disciplinary action before a student returns to classes. Counselors, interventionists, or other support staff might conduct a circle to help aid in a conflict resolution situation. In all of the aforementioned situations, some level of discord necessitated the creation of the circle.

At its core, a circle is a safe place to listen and be heard with a common goal. Teachers can initiate a circle where there is no conflict in order to foster connection for the classroom community. This doesn't have to be a deep soul stirring, staring into each other's eyes type of experience. Let's be real. Kids will not cooperate with that, and you don't have time for that anyway. It can simply be a time when you play a game of "Would You Rather" or ask a silly question and let students respond. You probably already do something like this.

The intentionality of the circle allows only one person to speak at a time by including a talking piece and because of the inevitable limited time for this activity, does not allow for rebuttals. In the virtual world, this can be accomplished by the oh so power-ful mute button. You listen and you learn about each person from their own lips.

Some fun variations to the circle might be telling a story from your youth and having students give you "advice" as though they were your friends at that age. To foster listening, you can write a collaborative story having each student add only one sentence. The benefits of a circle can easily spill over into other important marks that you are leaving.

When I meet with students in a group setting, they have been referred for a variety of reasons. In my general social skills groups, one skill that is significantly lacking is the skill of listening. In all honesty, this is not only true of those students. It is true of many of us adults as well. We listen to one another for as long as we can before excitedly interrupting to drop our pearls of wisdom. We listen only enough to respond. The circle can help grow the skill of listening because there is not an opportunity for rebuttal.

What I see with many students is that they don't just interrupt. They zone out. Having learned proper classroom etiquette, they wouldn't dare interrupt a classmate's story of what they did this weekend. That doesn't mean they are listening though. Many of them are taking their own mental vacations. You know this already. It becomes painfully obvious when they ask you what they are supposed to do after you have explained it three to five times already.

For students with this listening difficulty, I teach them to listen and respond. In pairs or groups of three at the most, students are given a beach ball which acts as a talking piece. The student who is chosen to speak first begins by holding the beach ball. When they are finished speaking, they volley it to the other person who asks a follow-up question or makes a related statement. The game continues in this way. They are only able to change the subject as it is related to the discussion. This helps alleviate those talkers like myself from monopolizing a conversation by "chasing rabbits," and it keeps the listener engaged. The goal is for both people to participate in the conversation. It creates a win-win situation. In our new contactless world, you can substitute a hand signal for the beach ball toss that the student gives when they are finished talking. You can include a timer to help keep the discussion flowing,

Conversations in the classroom can't always be "get to know you" friendly, and they don't only have to focus on the academic subject matter. These activities are versatile. Does your class need a break? Introduce a silly question. Are you needing to make the most of their learning and possibly conduct an informal assessment? Present them with a content related question. If they are working in pairs, ask them to report out their partner's answer for an extra challenge of application. Leaving the mark of listening can be done. We just need to take a moment to intentionally plan for opportunities to listen.

CHAPTER REFLECTIONS

In this chapter on "Listening," what was most impactful for you?

_____

_____

_____

What steps will you take to make certain that your students feel "heard" and ultimately appreciated in your classroom?

_____

_____

_____

What tools could you use to aid you or your students in being better listeners?

_____

_____

_____

THE MARK OF EMPOWERMENT

~Rufus~

Empowered teachers empower students.
                                    – Katie Martin

As educators, you have been given the gift of opportunity. Every day you have before you the opportunity to empower your student charges. That speaks of something that is far greater, longer lasting, and more impactful than academic student achievements. Students can leave your class empowered for life in a way they never thought possible.

A great friend of mine and fellow speaker, Joy Carter, related this story of Dr. Cheryl Jamison, an educator in the Atlanta Public Schools.

Dr. Jamison is a most extraordinary Special Ed teacher for at-risk kids in Atlanta. Her commitment to empowerment screams loudly as she is validated by student successes. Dr. Jamison focuses on her students' natural abilities while building up their weaker talents.

For emotion control and self-management, she teaches her students to knit and then encourages knitting in class as a coping mechanism. She teaches students how to think, not what to think. In so doing, to her great satisfaction and that of her students, empowerment happens. It is said the proof of the pudding is in the eating. Consider these tasty results. Currently, she has two Special Education students on the honor roll and two in early college classes.

Your students will never ask to be empowered. But they soar when you do empower them. From power comes power. So, if the educator is to empower the students, it presumes that the educator is empowered by the desire to nurture young minds and set student trajectories for life.

Your challenge will be to become so end-game empowered that distractions don't dissuade you from your goals for your students. Distractions like district push-pull, poorly funded schools, or disagreeable parents can never be allowed to cause you to break stride toward the lofty goals you have set for your students. Now that you're empowered, what are some ways to empower your students? Here are strategies that will prove helpful:

1. Students often perform in an environment they feel they own. An idea that's been met with success by many educators is classroom ownership. You allow your students to name your classroom. The name of the room must have some positive focus. That is the only caveat. Once it's named, make certain that class name appears prominently in your class. If the name has been chosen well, it will both empower and provide a sense of achievement for your students.

2. Showcase exemplary effort on more involved assignments. Just like adults, when students are aware that their work will be shared with fellow students, they will put more effort into presenting their very best.

3. Get to know your students better. Learn what motivates them, what excites them. Figure out a way to incorporate those interests as a part of your instruction. Because getting to know your students is such a powerful tool in leaving enduring marks, you will see the idea repeated throughout this book.

Business professional, Althea Ford, remembers this empowering story of one of her teachers:

I will always admire and respect Mrs. Walker. Mrs. Walker was my 5th grade teacher and at my current age of 46, I can still remember sitting in her classroom as if it were yesterday. I liked everything about Mrs. Walker's class, from the way we would sing our morning welcome song to the way we ended the day with story time. But most of all, it was what Mrs. Walker did in between those hours that made the biggest difference. Mrs. Walker was a teacher that looked past her students' flaws and saw the potential that was within. She knew when our work was our best, and when it wasn't our best. She encouraged us to do better, but she never judged or belittled.

I will never forget turning in my first essay. Mrs. Walker told me that I was a great writer and encouraged me to participate in a contest. I didn't want to disappoint Mrs. Walker, so I immediately got to work on it and submitted my draft. A couple of days later, I was informed that I had won first place. That was the beginning of a great love that I have for words and writing. Mrs. Walker saw a potential in me that I didn't know existed.

Because Mrs. Walker had confidence in me, I now have confidence in myself. Thank you, Mrs. Walker, for bringing out one of my best characteristics.

In this account, Mrs. Walker recognized excellence in Althea's ability to express herself impactfully in her use of words. It is interesting to note that Althea lived so close to her greatness, she couldn't see it. If teachers are to be ones who will empower, then they will

49

also have to be sensitive to the signs their students display. For some of your students, you will function as an "eye opener" as you point them to their greatness.

For Althea, the sign was writing. In others, it could be leadership skills, planning, or relationship building. Whatever it happens to be, the empowering teacher needs to find a way to highlight it and its benefits to the student who is unaware. Remember, we often live too close to our own greatness to be able to see it.

The following are actions that any educator can take to help empower their students:

1. **Provide positive reinforcement regularly**
   Students love to be praised for some accomplishment. I am convinced that there is nothing like a teacher looking a student squarely in the eyes and telling them about their particular greatness. Being specific really makes the acknowledgment even more special.

2. **Encourage creative expression**
   While it is necessary to clearly define the assignment lines that your students should paint between, it can be rather empowering when you sometimes allow them to "paint outside the lines." New abilities may emerge that empower your students, enabling them to handle future challenges.

3. **Help students find their passions**

If you were to ask your students what their passions are, they would likely not come up with anything definitive. They might even point to hobbies or entertainment. Spend time with your students to help them learn what drives them. It could be something that is easily seen like some artistic talent. Other times, it may be something hidden beneath the surface. Those will take more time to discover, but it is well worth the effort.

Sometimes you will have to call it as you see it when it comes to the student's passive greatness. Business professional, Robert Brown, relates this story from his Philadelphia Public School education process:

Ms. Sporanza had us write a short story at the start of the school year to see the nature of our writing skills. She gave me a "left-handed compliment" by saying to me, "You can write. You're just lazy!" I said something to myself like, "Oh no, she didn't" because I was surprised by that statement coming from my teacher! I decided to show her I was not lazy and learned everything she had to say about how to write and made use of it. Ms. Sporanza became one of my best teachers.

The skills of speaking and writing have served me well in furthering my education, earning a living, and sharing ideas with others. I have passed these skills on to my children, who are doing quite well, and I will always be grateful to teachers like Ms. Barbara Sporanza.

4. Share inspiring stories

Share empowering stories of other students who succeed in life. The plan here is that the student would see himself/herself in the story. That shifted vision would empower the student to believe beyond their current circumstances.

A true case in point on this empowerment is a story from two generations ago. Connie's words about inspiring students hits home for me. During my speaking presentations, I often relate my family's story. A recently single mom with five children (four boys and one girl) teaching all over rural Georgia had all the potential to end on a sad note. Instead, my mother ended her career as a 35-year educator, who nurtured and raised two educators, an educator/congressman, a businessman/professional speaker, and a telecommunications technician. She inspired her students and her children to do well through the life lessons she taught. Her teaching has rippled through generations now. Audiences often tell me our story resonated with them. Remind your students that now is not the end of their stories.

5. Allow for second chances

"Do overs" can be of great value with some

students. We have all functioned beneath our abilities or run at right angles to some assignment we were given. When it crashes and burns, we must be fully aware that we are the culprits and own the associated shame.

It can be incredibly empowering when a gifted teacher sees the student as better than the offense and gives them a second chance. Sometimes there is a metamorphosis that takes place that amazes even the gifted teacher. Appreciating the "second chance," a more empowered student emerges. That empowerment will have future-forward impact.

6. Ask for what you want

Teach proactivity. Beyond your classroom, waiting in the distance, is an often resistant world that will need to be challenged into submission. In short, your students will have to ask for what they want. This concept will be better understood with 5th graders and beyond. They should understand that nothing will ever be handed to them.

They should present themselves as someone of value and then ask for what they want. Teach your students the value of resilience. Your students should appreciate the benefit of "hanging in there." There will always be something that wants to trip them up.

They should understand that the longer they hold on, the longer they *can* hold on. You as the educator should determine if this concept is beyond your students' level of comprehension.

There is nothing like the unknown to generate fear and a depreciation of confidence. Once your students understand what awaits them, they are much more empowered and ready for the confrontations they face. That "confrontation" may be as simple as the next assignment or an encounter on the playground, but with confidence, they will be able to negotiate it.

CHAPTER REFLECTIONS

In this chapter on "Empowerment," what was most impactful for you?

_____

_____

_____

To appreciate the effect of empowerment, what has empowerment meant to you in your life?

_____

_____

_____

What tools of empowerment will you use to assist your students?

_____

_____

_____

THE MARK OF CARING

~Rufus~

*Students don't care how much you know
until they know how much you care.*
— John C. Maxwell

Educational studies have led researchers to believe that caring relationships with teachers help students do better in school and, in turn, treat others kinder. Many of us are the happy beneficiaries of actively caring teachers and school administrators.

The possibilities abound around ways of extending care to your students. Consider this caring story shared by education professional LaVerne Hamilton, a retired Principal from Duval County in Florida.

Nearly every day one Afro-American 4th grader was perpetually late to school. He would be involved in a fight after leaving school. It is important to say in 2001 "paddling" was a way of life in his school. He appeared before me once to be paddled. Since I took a stand that no paddling would take place in the school, we often spent time talking. I learned he and his sister lived with their eighty-year-old grandmother. They came to school whenever they were awakened. That was an easy fix. I bought an alarm clock and taught him how to use it.

His mother was somewhere on drugs. He didn't know his father. He came to school in dirty clothes smelling of urine. He apparently had not been to a barber in a long time. A home visit made it clear they needed help.

So once a month my daughter and I would take the family to the laundromat. On that same Saturday, I would get Willie's haircut and his sister's hair done. My daughter and I went shopping to buy some additional changes of clothes. The fights stopped and frequency of office visits were reduced. It was all about the new respect they received.

However, change occurred when the grandmother started showing signs of dementia. Her son placed the children in foster care to address his mother's needs.

The story did not end as I hoped. I learned a few years later that Willie's sister was adopted, and

Willie was in the juvenile system. While I don't know today's outcome for them, I do know they had a time of feeling good about themselves. At that time, they no longer walked around with targets on their backs. They walked with self-respect.

While the story did not end as Mrs. Hamilton had hoped, her intentionality was clearly on display. She engaged the student's situation with an inclined heart focused on "Willie."

Education Director of the Greater Good Science Center, Vicki Zakrzewski Ph.D., wrote:

If I asked you to tell me what you remembered most about your favorite teacher growing up, I bet you wouldn't say much about the subject matter. Instead, I'd expect you to describe how he or she made you feel as you learned that subject matter—the sense of excitement or discovery you felt, or the safety to take chances and make mistakes, or the confidence that you were valued as a human being, warts and all.

*According to research, few factors in education have a greater impact on a student's educational experience than a **caring relationship with his or her teacher.***

There are both rich and far-reaching consequences that attend the steps of an intentionally caring educator. So, having settled the issue on the benefits of a caring teacher, let's consider some of the how-to points around caring.

Research has identified practical tips for teachers to help them build caring relationships with students. Consider the ones listed below:

1. **Make it an objective to know your students and the lives they lead.**
   This is especially important if your students are from a different cultural or socio-economic background than you. Research has proven that when teachers visit the homes of their students, they gain a deeper awareness of their students. They are better able to help them and extend genuine care.

2. **Seek to get feedback from your students.**
   On the subject of your choice, ask your students to tell you how they express their feelings around that subject, how it makes them feel. When you allow for feedback and actually consider it, you let your students know that what they say matters in your class and that they are valued. Your students will also feel safe to ask questions, no matter how "dumb." This will assist them in their ability to learn.

3. **Actively engage and listen to your students.**
   When you actively listen to your student, you open yourself to understand your student while

confirming that your student heard what was said to him/her.

A teacher who actively listens to students is listening for the meaning *behind* what students are saying, then checks in with them to make sure the student was understood correctly. This act of listening strengthens your student's self-image and solidifies the relationship you're attempting to build. Choose places that allow for complete concentration and are without noisy or visual distractions.

As teachers, we often don't realize how even the smallest caring gesture can have a huge impact on our students. As evidence, I'd like to share the story of Sam, a high school student from south central Los Angeles who had transferred high schools three times before being interviewed by researchers for a study.

After years of feeling uncared for in school, Sam was very surprised when he received a phone call at home from his current school's office, wanting to know why he was absent that day. His other schools, he said, never called to check on him. A small act of caring—but here's how Sam said it made him feel:

When they call my house if I'm not [at school], they're real friendly. My auntie has an answering machine, and sometimes I'll hear a voice start to leave a message like "Hi, Sam. If you're there, we're wondering why you're not in school today . . ." If I hear that, I pick up the phone and explain why I'm not there. And they believe me. They trust me, so I trust them.

As writers of this book, we believe that you, as teachers, came equipped for the challenge of leaving "caring" marks. You knowingly entered into this teaching profession driven by a desire to impact young minds. Your efforts will prompt them toward great life trajectories. It was your heart that brought you into this reality, and it will be your heart that will empower you to impact well and to leave great marks of caring.

CHAPTER REFLECTIONS

In this chapter on "Caring," what was most impactful for you?

_____

_____

_____

Is caring something that is easily seen by your students? If not, how will you modify your interfaces with your students to reflect that you do care?

_____

_____

_____

How will you remind yourself of the critical importance of leaving the mark of caring on your students?

_____

_____

_____

THE MARK OF BELONGING

~Connie~

Those who have a strong sense of love and belonging
have the courage to be imperfect.
— Brené Brown

Who are your people? We have many groups that encompass our people. We are members of professional groups, family groups, church groups, and friend groups. In each of these areas of our lives, we are part of something where everybody knows our name, and we know their names as well. There is a purpose for each of these groups. There is a name for each of these groups. There are even specific foods and inside jokes associated with these groups. "Your people" is a way of describing a group to which you belong.

You need not look far to find evidence that this current generation, despite the swell of social media options, is one the loneliest generations to date. Is it because there are too few ways to connect socially or too few YouTube channels to which you can sub-scribe? We're sure you know that the answer is a resounding "No." It has been said that it is possible to be in a crowded room and still be alone. Belonging is not a matter of simply achieving membership. It is deeper.

Many of our students find themselves as part of groups to which they do not belong. A classroom can be a place where all of the students belong.

I look back on my middle school years and the years that I taught middle school as confusing times for students. These are the times when you begin to determine who your people are. You may come to middle school with your friend group fully intact or go to middle school having to create your group from scratch. Either way, thanks to hormones and puberty, it can be an interesting time. Some students even go to middle school thinking that they know who their people are only to have it shift. Middle school is at some point a search for belonging.

My daughter and I recently revisited her entrance to middle school. She shared with me that her love of reading brought her to a place of solace during her friendship transition. She noticed during 6th grade that her former friend group began to shape shift, leaving her in search of who her people were.

Recess became the most necessary time to have a group. Because of her love for reading, she would frequently use recess time to retreat to the library. It was there that she and another student with whom she was acquainted weathered the storm of friendship uncertainty.

The librarian allowed these girls to find refuge in a book. From time to time, she would engage the students in conversation, sharing her knowledge of books and their shared interests. This librarian, though not desiring to create her own place of belonging, was able to provide that much needed space for these young girls. As the year progressed, my daughter spent less and less time in the library although her love for reading in no way diminished. When I asked why, she said that she had begun to develop substantial friendships and had found her people. It was the time spent in the library that provided a safe haven and developed her confidence to inevitably find her place of belonging.

The Purpose of Belonging

Middle School is not the only place that a search for belonging takes place. It takes place every year as school begins. Most students start the year in a classroom with a new teacher and classmates who range in familiarity from close friends to total strangers. There are many studies that focus on the effects of teachers looping with their students from one grade level to the next.

Some of the arguments for looping are the continued camaraderie, the increase in academic rigor, and the development of culture and belonging. Not having to learn the personalities and names of a whole new group of students is helpful especially during difficult times. When we ended the in-person school year in March of 2020, we were faced with uncertainty. As we began to plan for the next school year, we chose not to loop teachers but to have students stay in their grouping from the previous year. Not re-pitching classes (changing the class assignments) was one of our first plans to help manage these new confusing and unprecedented times. This fostered a sense of belonging.

One of my favorite ways to focus on belonging is to take a personality test. When our campus took the DISC personality test, I got a kick out of discovering what my strengths were and guessing where my colleagues fell on the DISC. As part of our work around this new tool, we were grouped with those whom we worked most closely. In the leadership team of just three at that time, we represented all four areas of the DISC. It was apparent to me in our discussion that I had strengths that the other members of my group did not, and likewise, they had strengths that I did not. This discovery made me want to work with them more. It made me feel like a member of the dream team. I felt like I belonged.

I was so pumped that I took my enthusiasm into the

classroom with kid-friendly personality tests. My daughter and I bonded over this, and she even found one for everyone in our family to complete. My work friends and I even joke over coffee about the purpose that we each serve in our group.

At first glance, these quizzes are fun to learn about ourselves, but in the context of your group, it explains your purpose and creates a deeper sense of belonging. There is nothing that I hate more than being without a purpose. I don't really do small talk well. It is when I am sitting in a room of people who are anything less than my inner circle, without something to do, that I feel like I don't belong the most. It is why I often wait until the absolute last moment to arrive at events. I intentionally seek to avoid that awkward "what do I do now" feeling. However, even in a room of strangers, I can eliminate that feeling if I have a purpose.

As educators, we can help our students develop a sense of belonging by assigning tasks throughout the lesson such as table leaders, classroom jobs, or simply explaining the active listening expectations for the class. Everyone wants to belong, and establishing a purpose is one way to accomplish the task.

I Belong to Me

In order to truly belong, you have to be authentically you. That is something that students may struggle with as they get older. Once they begin to realize that others aren't perfect, they realize the same is true of themselves. They may feel as though they must assimilate in order to belong in a group. The greatest lesson of belonging that we must teach is the lesson of belonging to yourself.

Michael de Montaigne said, "The greatest thing in the world is to know how to belong to oneself." It is once we realize that we must first belong to ourselves, flaws and all, that we become comfortable enough in our own skin so that we feel we belong any and everywhere we go.

This is, of course, a process, not something that we can teach in a lesson. It's not even something we can model for our students in a single school year. Instead, it is a subtle and continual practice that we must encourage and foster in the lives of our students, year after year. We continue to build upon the foundations that have been laid by our colleagues in previous years.

One way to foster the gift of true belonging that is found in self-acceptance is through championing our students. Everyone needs a champion. If you have taught even for a little while, you know that not every student has one. Being a champion while not compromising accountability is crucial. Championing brings confidence.

As a mother, I began to understand this even more

as my own children got older. I recently upended my sending out recitation of everything from "have a good day" to "make good choices" as my kids left for school. I would usually end that laundry list with "make me proud" or "make God proud" before kissing them on the head and sending them off to school. It was only after I realized how self-serving those statements are that I thought better of their use. Ultimately, those messages say "don't embarrass me." I sent a similar message to my 5th graders during my first year of teaching as they headed off to P.E., Art, or Music. Those "well wishes" are not from a place of pride in the student or even trust in their ability to make the right decision for the myriad of choices that they will face before they return to my firm grasp and watchful eye.

Those statements and ones like them are about how their behavior will reflect upon me. This creates a burden only making the weight of anxiety heavier while doing nothing to build confidence or self-acceptance.

I have now begun to say, "Make yourself proud." Admittedly not something I might say to a class of six year olds, but the message is appropriate for middle school, high school, and even upper elementary. At this point they know what will make you proud or displeased, but have they thought about the effect of their actions on themselves beyond the trouble they might get into? This stance sends the message of trust and helps them really get in touch with who they are. They begin to realize the effects of their choices and explore what specific choices mean for them.

Bit by bit they are learning about the boy or girl within them and what it feels like to belong to him or her. If we can teach students to belong to themselves, they will realize they belong everywhere. They will dream those dreams and tackle the obstacles that they are destined to conquer. Belonging begins within and then spreads outward. As educators, we have the unique privilege of being able to shape it at every stage.

CHAPTER REFLECTIONS

*Where do you **most** experience "Belonging" as discussed in this chapter?*

_____

_____

_____

What are two ways that you can foster a sense of belonging for your students, both to the group and to themselves as individuals?

_____

_____

_____

How will you remind yourself of the critical importance of leaving the mark of belonging on your students?

_____

_____

_____

THE MARK OF SAFETY

~Rufus~

Students learn best when they feel welcomed,
comfortable, and SAFE.
    – Mrs. Blackwell, Kindergarten Teacher

Safety is defined as *"the condition of being protected from or unlikely to cause danger, risk, or injury."* In a school in South Holland, Illinois, the building principal gave a daily early morning welcome to the students. After completing a whole list of things that would be happening that day and some of the expectations she had for the students, she finished by saying very convincingly, "You are safe here." The perception of safety is a key element to the success of the students' learning process.

A friend shared the story of a student named Mateo. He had experienced behavioral problems since kindergarten. His 2nd grade year was an extremely difficult time for him. His school's support staff found themselves spending a lot of time with him that year.

As his 2nd grade year came to a close, his new teachers began to prepare for his arrival to their classrooms in the fall. They were aware of his frequent time out of the classroom. They worked with their colleagues who were most familiar with Mateo's needs and came up with a plan for his success in their classrooms.

In his 3rd grade year, Mateo wasn't seen as often by administrators and support staff. One day he asked his teacher if he could go and speak with the school counselor. She allowed him to go. Some of the school's staff worked with him to help him regulate his emotions. He understood that when things in the class got too overwhelming and he felt strong emotions coming on, he could ask to remove himself. His teachers were aware of this self-management tool and encouraged his use of it. On this particular day, when Mateo returned from the counselor's office, his class was at recess. Before joining his peers on the playground, Mateo stopped to check in with his teacher. His teacher responded by praising him for choosing to take a break. She mentioned that it seemed to her to be a pretty good year for him, and she asked him if he thought so too. After a short pause, he said, "Yeah."

Pleased to hear this, his teacher told him she was glad about this and asked him what he thought made this year better. Mateo gave her a little smile and responded, "You . . . you make me feel safe." Taken aback, his teacher didn't say anything at first. Then she smiled, thanked him, and told him she was glad he was in her class.

Now, it was unlikely that Mateo's teachers were purposefully cultivating "safety" in their classrooms. As in any school, the teachers know who the "frequent flyers" to the office are. They knew Mateo's history. "Safe" was not likely the feeling the teachers were trying to cultivate in him as they planned and strategized to help him have a successful year. It probably had more to do with calm. But here's the huge takeaway! The safety Mateo experienced in the classroom allowed him not to act out. It caused him to feel that he was safe there, and he didn't have to be disruptive.

One goal for most teachers is to have students remain in class as much as possible. In this case, because Mateo felt safe, his disruptions were almost non-existent, and he spent the much needed time in the classroom. His answer to his teacher resonated with her, and she no doubt will cherish his words. I'm sure she couldn't wait to relay them it to his other awesome teacher. Together they had set the environment for safety, even unwittingly.

As you read this chapter, we want this story to

resonate with you as well. We challenge you to intentionally produce rooms that give off safety vibes to all of your students.

You can't possibly know all of the abuses, both verbal and physical, that visit your students with great regularity. There may be other issues that cause your students to feel uneasy on a daily basis. Things like playground extortion and intense teasing can cause your students to scream for a safe harbor.

Because you don't know all that they face, you can't appreciate what your intentionally constructed environment of safety may mean to them. The intentional teacher has to be preemptive. You must assume an on-going need for an atmosphere of safety.

Consider the following action plans that can assist you in providing an atmosphere of safety in the classroom:

1. **Display students' work**
   Students love to see their assignments posted in the class. There is a sense of student ownership of the room. It is more meaningful for the students to see their "stuff" rather than some purchased poster.

2. **Admit when you don't know**
   Students seldom see teachers as capable of making mistakes. They really appreciate seeing

that you are human just like they are. It pays great dividends in the appreciation of your students for your integrity and the overall class environment.

3. **Remain calm at all times**
   Once a teacher loses it with a class or student, it takes a long time to rebuild that feeling of safety and trust within those four walls. Step right outside the door and take a few breaths. It's worth it.

4. **Take every opportunity to model kindness**
   They will embrace your model.

5. **Share your vulnerability**
   They will appreciate this. What's good for the goose is good for the gander. If we are asking kids to write and talk about times when they have felt scared, alone, confused, or angry, we need to be willing to do the same.

6. **Smile often**
   Genuine smiles are priceless. They prepare the way for relationship development, and they communicate the idea of safety. Smiles are self-generating. You get as you give. Students will respond often and enthusiastically. Students can see your smile, even through your COVID mask.

7. **Laugh with your students**
   Mark Twain said, "Against the assault of laughter,

nothing can stand." Laughter neutralizes the tensions that often attend the process of learning. Seeing a teacher fully involved in laughter along with the class can be an eye opener. Students will see these teachers who can laugh with them differently and appreciated them more. It will help them feel secure. Once again, teachers can reveal their humanness in the happiness of laughter.

It is our sincere wish that all of your students, like Mateo, feel wonderfully safe in the learning space that you so intentionally construct.

CHAPTER REFLECTIONS

In this chapter on "Safety," what was most impactful for you?

_____

_____

_____

On a scale of 1 to 10, 10 being the safest, how safe do you think your students would rank your classroom?

_____

_____

_____

Which of the suggested methodologies in this chapter will you use to produce the atmosphere of safety in your classroom?

_____

_____

_____

THE HILL YOU'VE CHOSEN

*The only limits to your impact are your
imagination and commitment.*
                        – Anthony Robbins

Of the thousands of career paths available to you, you have chosen the one that affects millions. As the opening quote so aptly put it, *"Teachers make all other professions possible."* You come with keen-eyed focus, stiffened spines, and hearts inclined toward significantly impacting your students.

We have talked at length about leaving marks and their effects and their long range potential impact. You have heard a lot of what you likely already knew but perhaps had forgotten or not thought about for a while. Education! This is the hill on which you have chosen to plant your flag.

You have done the heavy lifting of qualifying your-self academically. In fact, many of you have returned to the academic well for additional buckets of graduate and post-graduate preparation. You have sharpened your skills by working with journeyman educators who knew where the land mines were buried.

You have made mistakes that made and still make you blush even today. You have run interference for many who desperately needed your intervention. You have endured rebukes from your superiors for blurring the lines of convention. Some child had a need, and your heart wouldn't let you sit quietly in the face of glaring suffering. You moved, you helped, and you paid for it.

You agree to rise early for school and return home late with the activities of the day still singing in your head. At times, even though you don't want to, you re-visit the emotions that rattled you earlier that day. You can still see the angry tilt of your student's mother's head as she lost herself in an unreasonable rant. You couldn't wait until the close of the day or at least until she left your room.

As difficult as some days and some experiences can be, their noise was often softened, and sometimes blotted out entirely, by an unexpected intervention.

You would hear a sweeter sound in the distance, perhaps while at the supermarket. You'd hear the familiar voice of a student who had been in your class some time ago. You never realized your impact on her until she runs over to you beaming.

Before you know it, she has given you a hug and is introducing you to her grandfather. Speaking to her grandfather, she squeals, "Papa, she is the best teacher EVER!"

That's why you do what you do! That's the hill you've chosen. **We are all better for your choice!**

Something to Think About

"Almost everything will work again if you unplug it for a few minutes, including you." – *Anne Lamott*

"Education is the most powerful weapon which you can use to change the world." – *Nelson Mandela*

"Teacher? I prefer the term Educational Rockstar." – *Unknown*

"Teacher: Where is your homework? Me: I lost it fighting this kid who said you weren't the best teacher in the school." – *Corey Booker*

"The art of teaching is the art of assisting discovery." – *Mark Van Doren*

"Every child deserves a champion—an adult who will never give up on them, who understands the power of connection and insists that they become the best that they can possibly be." – *Rita Pierson*

"Teachers are expected to reach unattainable goals with inadequate tools. The miracle is that at times they accomplish this impossible task." – *Haim Ginott*

"The teacher's task is to initiate the learning process and then get out of the way." – *John Warren*

"A teacher affects eternity; he [or she] can never tell where his [or her] influence stops." – *Henry B. Adams*

"In teaching you cannot see the fruit of a day's work. It is invisible and remains so, maybe for twenty years." – *Jacques Barzun*

ABOUT THE AUTHOR

Constance S. Johnson, M.Ed.
Certified School Counselor

Constance, affectionately known as Connie, grew up in a suburb outside Chicago, Illinois. She has wanted to teach for as long as she can remember. She can even recall playing school being one of her favorite things to do as a young child.

Seeking to accomplish her goal, she graduated from Tuskegee University with a B.S. in Elementary Education. Later, her heart required that she equip herself with new ways to help her students work through traumas and become their greatest selves. So, she returned to the "well" to get her M.Ed. in School Counseling from the University of West Alabama.

She has worked in the field of education for 16 years and is in her seventh year as an elementary school counselor. When she is not dreaming up ways to impact her students, she enjoys spending time with family and friends.

ABOUT THE AUTHOR

Rufus D. Stephens
Motivational Speaker and Author

Rufus Stephens is a product of the Chatham County (Savannah) Georgia public school system. His mother and his aunt were excellent educators there. Both taught him in grade school on separate occasions. He developed a healthy respect for teachers early in his life.

He completed his undergraduate degree at Savannah State University and engaged in graduate studies at the University of Florida. He is a former business executive, business owner, and most currently a professional speaker and ordained minister.

As a speaker he "lives to impact"! He speaks to audiences in both virtual and in-person settings across the country. At age 72, he maintains he's just hitting his stride. He maintains that *"Life is a book that we all get to write. We don't know when the story ends, so we ought to let the pen fly."*

In March of 2020, he released his book *Life Lessons from Miss Mattie* to rave reviews. This book chronicles the life of his teacher-mother, Mattie Stephens. It highlighted eight of the life lessons she taught her children as she prepared them for life.

He looks upon the co-authoring of this book with his daughter, Connie, as a labor of love. He has plans for additional books and looks forward to engaging audiences both now and in a post COVID-19 America.

Made in the USA
Columbia, SC
28 July 2021